P9-APT-974

BY FOR *Actors, Actors*

A collection of original
MONOLOGUES & SCENES

Volume 1

Edited by
CATHERINE GAFFIGAN

Excalibur Publishing
New York

LIBRARY
ST. LOUIS COMMUNITY COLLEGE
AT FLORISSANT VALLEY

© 1991 Excalibur Publishing
All rights reserved. This book, or parts thereof, may not
be reproduced in any form without permission.
Copyrights on individual monologues and scenes are
retained by the respective authors.

All material in this volume may be used freely for
audition, workshop and classroom purposes. A royalty
is required for all public performances. Contact the
publisher for details and rates.

Published by:
Excalibur Publishing
434 Avenue of the Americas, Suite 790
New York, NY 10011

Cover design: Peter J. Byrnes

Library of Congress Card Catalogue Number: 91-74160

ISBN 0-9627226-2-6

Printed in the United States of America

Table of Contents

INTRODUCTION

Wise selection of monologues, combined with solid preparation, will ensure that your audience, be it one agent or twelve hundred paying customers, will be totally absorbed by your performance. To select material suitable for yourself, and to perform it well, the following is what you need to know, and what you need to do:

About the Monologue Itself

Any monologue that you select for yourself speaks volumes about how you see yourself and how well you know yourself — or how little you know yourself. So you are communicating even before you start to "act" the monologue.

The basic rule to follow is: you serve the material, the material serves you. Who you *are* should illuminate the text. This means that your monologues should be a good fit with whatever age, size, shape and color you are in real life: your unique combination of traits and talents.

Choosing appropriate material is equally crucial if you are presenting yourself doing "character" work. If you want the casting people to know that you can play a 12-year-old or an 80-year-old, you should choose a monologue that lends itself to that concept; that is to say, the character traits are written into the text and not superimposed by you. Examples include Frankie in *The Member of the Wedding*, Richard in *Ah, Wilderness*, the Grandmother in *The American Dream*, or Nonno in *The Night of the Iguana*. Otherwise, you might end up doing your character work the way it's done in high school — you know, with white shoe polish in your hair!

A monologue should be inherently dramatic and intriguing in and of itself. For this requirement to be met, you must have a talented colleague in the writer.

We speak of monologues as "acting alone," but you are never up there by yourself. If you choose a strongly written piece of material, the writer is up there with you.

Of course, a gifted performer can deliver the most banal material in a highly diverting way. Imagine Robin Williams, Billy Crystal or Whoopi Goldberg performing the telephone directory! If you are not similarly gifted or are uncertain about the quality and suitability of your monologue choices, seek guidance.

When you are reading through material searching for monologues, certain pieces will just *reach* you. Work with such monologues. Your gut reaction means that you know something about what is written, and *that* connection gives you a head start on the monologue work. And, by the way, you don't have to understand *why* you like it so much.

Whatever your final choices, be sure that you feel very good about what you choose and what you do, rather than being focused on "do they *like* it?" or "do they *like me.*"

About Your Preparation

To perform a monologue well, you should already have some training and experience in scene work. The reason for this is that you use everything that you do in scene work when you do a monologue. And, of course, you have to do *all* the work. You (obviously) do not have a partner to carry some of the responsibility. With solid training, you are equipped to harness the text, rather than being swamped by it.

Here's how to proceed:

1) Know the text absolutely perfectly (this requires hundreds of repetitions) and be able to repeat it without a desperate search for the next thought. If, instead, you are grappling with the text, you communicate a tug-of-war between your memory

and your nerves. Such ineptitude *becomes* the drama, and the monologue itself is eclipsed. The audience very quickly gets focused on: "Oh, my God, will s/he get through it?"

2) Have a very strong objective in the fictional life of the monologue. This objective is separate and distinct from your objective of getting the job!

3) Know who you are talking to in the fiction. In acting technique, this is called **defining the relationship**. You define a relationship by asking yourself, "how does this person make me *feel*?"

4) Once you have defined the relationship, do a **recall** on that definition. A recall is an exercise that Stanislavski called an **emotional memory**. You should learn how to do this in a class. If you do not know how to do a recall, just sit, relax, breathe deeply and think of a person in your life you would tell this story to and how that person makes you feel.

5) Fill in the text. Make specific substitutions for words, phrases and references in the monologue to actual events in your life. For instance, if the monologue contains the phrase "my glamorous Aunt Mary," substitute the thought of a real person who you have known who is/was glamorous, but who is not necessarily a relative. She wears a lot of jewelry, for instance, or crazy hats.

and lastly,

6) Rehearse the monologue until you do it with ease, pleasure and the enjoyment of performing.

Where Do You Go From Here

A well-prepared monologue is a stepping stone to employment *and* gives you another chance to act. Your presentation should be a combination of pride and humility in "showing your wares": the trademarks of a real pro!

Remember, your monologues are your own "star package." In this book, and in subsequent volumes, it is our intention to provide you with exceptional and original monologues for use at auditions. Well prepared, these monologues will enhance your career opportunities.

Almost every monologue in this volume is true — it actually happened in someone's life. And so, with each selection, you begin with the strength and integrity of the poetry of the human heart. Stage directions only appear where clarification seems needed; they have been kept to an absolute minimum to give your imagination free reign.

One last thought: keep in mind that a well-prepared monologue takes about three months of work, so the best time to work on a monologue is when you *don't need one.* You must get the monologue into your body, voice and psyche, much as a singer absorbs and possesses a song. If you sing, you understand this concept, and a monologue is really a song without the musical accompaniment.

You should have at least two monologues fully prepared *before* pursuing auditions. Begin with two contemporary pieces, one serious and one comic. Ultimately, you should have a total of four monologues at your command, the two contemporary pieces plus two Shakespeare pieces, also one serious and one comic. With these in your arsenal, you are ready for all casting calls, and you can mix and match as circumstances require.

About the Scenes

We have included five brand new two-person scenes. These are intended for the audition circumstance where scenes, in addition to or instead of monologues, are welcome. (Yes, it happens occasionally.) They are also excellent classroom exercises or performances pieces. (For permission to use either the scenes or monologues in performance, contact the publisher.)

Acknowledgments

We are deeply indebted to all the contributing writers whose work appears here, and I personally thank each one of them. Each contributing writer's generosity of spirit has made this volume possible.

In addition, I express my admiration and special thanks to Sharon Good. It has been a joy to work with her on this project.

An Invitation

If you wish to appear as a contributing author in our subsequent volumes, please refer to page 62 for instructions. We welcome your remembrances, your joys, your secret loves, your life's events. It's all drama — and that's what we need for Volume 2!

Break a leg!

Catherine Gaffigan
New York City, 1991

Monologues

A Vacation in Greece
by Leslie Reed Ferro

Have you heard of Spetses? It's a small island in Greece. It's beautiful! The streets are cobblestone, and there are no cars anywhere. Transportation is horse and carriage, bicycle, or on foot. I was there once on vacation with my family, but something awful happened, and I felt responsible; I was the oldest. Maybe you don't want to hear this; it's pretty gory.

Well, I was bike riding with my sisters, Diane and Robin. We were going pretty fast. I remember the wonderful cool breeze on my face. Robin said, "Let's race to the beach." So Diane pulled out ahead, and there was a horse and carriage coming from the opposite direction. Before I could do anything, there was a loud noise. It seemed so out of place, the sun was shining so strongly. My heart skipped a beat. I could see Diane's bicycle lying on its side on the cobblestones. I couldn't see her, but I could hear her voice. She kept repeating, "Mommy, I'm scared, Mommy, I'm scared."

And then I saw her. She had a big opening in her head, next to her eye, and it was all bloody. The carriage driver was saying things in Greek which I didn't understand. He picked Diane up and put her in the carriage. I climbed in and took her beautiful little head in my lap. The hole in her head was so big that I could see right into her head. Oh, God, I felt so responsible. I'm the oldest. Blood was smeared on my shorts and my thigh where her head rested. Robin yelled to me that she was going back to the hotel to get Mom and Dad. Diane was very frightened and kept repeating, "I want Mommy." I could see veins and blood, and I didn't want to look anymore. I was telling her, "Everything is going to be alright, sweetheart," but my heart felt heavy and my eyes were watery. I kept thinking, "This is my fault."

Finally, we got to a house. The carriage driver carried Diane inside. There was a man there. He looked like a doctor dressed in something that looked like a uniform. He spoke a little English. He said, "American?" I told him, "Yes, and my parents are at the Delphi Hotel." He said something to the nurse, and she called the hotel. I heard her say my parents' name. The doctor took Diane into another room, and she was repeating, "I want my Mommy." By this time, my heart was beating so fast, and I was crying. All I could think of was, "I'm the oldest, and I shouldn't have let this happen." Well, after about a half-hour, which seemed like a year, my parents came running in. They consulted with the doctor in the other room where Diane was, and my mother and Robin and I were sent back to the hotel in the carriage. I remember there was the smell of the blood, although the driver had tried to clean off the seat.

At the hotel, we found out that my father took Diane on a plane to a big hospital in Athens. Well, that was a long time ago. She still has the scar on the side by her left eye, and every time I see it, yes, it reminds me of Spetses, but also of how dear she is to me.

Politics
by Betty Bennett

Do you know that I actually met Cecil B. De Mille? I had just arrived in Hollywood with my vaudeville uncle, Joe. Uncle Joe had introduced me to the rudiments of comedy, and we had performed our comedy act in clubs and local theaters all over the South. Well, anyway, I had written a rather dramatic letter to Mr. De Mille. At least I thought it was dramatic. I told all about the comedy act and my uncle Joe and our club dates. I went to the Lux Radio Theatre parking lot. Remember the Lux Radio Theatre? So here I was, placing my letter on the seat of Mr. De Mille's open sedan when — lo and behold — here was Mr. De Mille himself, in person — alone — fetching his own car! I explained about my letter, and that I hoped to audition for him. He was most charming. He tipped his hat and thanked me. Can you imagine? I left the parking lot walking on air, and about three weeks later, I received a call from his office to come in for an audition. I was thrilled. I should tell you that in the meantime, Uncle Joe and I had auditioned at MGM, Paramount's rival. So anyway, the big day arrived, and I went to Mr. De Mille's office at Paramount to audition. I not-so-casually mentioned my audition at MGM to Mr. De Mille's assistant. She disappeared into the "big office." Well, I waited and waited, and finally, the assistant came back and told me the audition was cancelled. I forget what reason she gave. I never heard from Paramount again. I was very naive about the politics of Hollywood, but I know better now.

My Buddy, My Friend
by Sharon Good

I think you can never have friends the way you did when you were twelve. It seems impossible to find a real, simple, old-fashioned buddy anymore. When I was twelve, my best friend, my buddy, was Janet. We were a pair, total opposites. I was shy; she was wild. I was quiet, she was brash. She used to make things up and tell them to everyone as if they were the truth. Like, she used to tell people that she had a cousin in England who knew the Beatles, and that she talked to John and Paul on the phone all the time. She even invited me to stay over one night, saying that they would call about three in the morning. They never did, of course, and I didn't really care. I was surprised, though, to find out that she would lie even to me.

But she was a great friend. Whenever we both wanted something, like which game to play or the last chocolate cookie, she would always give in willingly and let me have it. And she taught me to play the guitar. She had learned in camp and came back and taught me. We would get together at her house and play folk songs in her bedroom, taking turns singing harmony. I wanted to enter the school talent show, but Janet wouldn't perform in public. "Oh, no," she said, "no way!"

Oh, and then there was that time we went fishing. There was a lake a few blocks from her house. In the garage, we found this net that belonged to her brother. We took it and walked down to the lake, took our shoes and socks off, and waded in up to our knees. Now you have to understand how ridiculous this was, fishing with a net. All we could find were minnows, about this big, and they swam right through the holes in the net. We kept hoping for something bigger, but nothing came, so finally we turned back toward the shore. About three feet in front of us was a foot-long catfish! I had the net, so I carefully moved in and scooped it up. We were thrilled! We walked home, so proud of ourselves, planning how we would have it for dinner. But Janet's mother didn't see it our way. She wouldn't let the filthy thing in the house. I called my mother, and she felt pretty much the same way. So we did the only thing left — we gave it a decent burial in the flower beds.

But Janet and I ended up in different junior high schools, and we began to drift apart. By the time we graduated from high school, we had become merely nodding acquaintances. I think it was more her choice than mine. I really missed her. A lot. I never really had another friend as special as Janet. She was one of a kind. Sometimes I still miss my buddy . . . I wonder where she is now.

Peter Dog: A Modern Morality
by Cynthia Hopkins

And do you, Peter Dog, take this Puss-Bitch to be thy lawful wedded Rat, and to live in infidelity for the rest of thy life? For the rest of Pain, for the rest of Love. Peter Dog is a blind man and a weak man. You may choose love if you wish, but surely it is better to choose the truth. "What's done can't be undone," Peter Dog used to say, and, "Stand by a principle until you find a better one. It's only God does not exist." Shame on you, Peter Dog.

Peter Dog and Pussy lived together for nine years, but Peter Dog was married to the Rat. Pussy and the Rat never spoke to one another; they were divided by the immorality of pain. The Rat said, "Only pain can make us live." But Peter Dog just pursed up his face and frowned in disapproval. "Old friends are for pleasure," he would sternly admonish. Pussy only purred. All she ever did was purr. The purring came from a bowl of cream. She lay curled up in a bowl of cream and licked with her tongue the tip of her tail. The Rat slunk off, in an ache of pain. "One must suffer to be pure, and in purity lies death. Death is the release," thought the sleek, ugly, shivering Rat, but she couldn't die. The purring Pussy-cat died in ecstasy each night, and like a phoenix bird rose up stretching from the fire, scratching on the hearthrug with her long, cruel nails. Peter Dog ruffled her fur with his lapping, rough tongue. He, too, enjoyed the warm, rich taste of cream. Sickly, dirty, poisoned cream. But Peter Dog didn't know; still less did he care.

Peter Dog was a simple dog . . . and so on and so forth . . . to hell with it!

Grief
by Chocolate Waters

My grief spills out upon the earth,
as endless as the journey of The Fool.
Of all the doubts that I have had
since leaping off the cliff that was my life,
Of all the deaths that I've been through
since landing in New York with just a suitcase
and my Scruff-o cat beside me —
No single one has broken my determination
to become my best of selves
like Scruff-o's death has cracked my walking stick
    in two.
Not the loss of all my lovers and my friends,
Not the loss of the city that harbored me a decade,
or the loss of humor, my muse,
Or the sidewalk sales of my possessions,
Or the theft of all my jewels.
So why should the death of this old, scruffie cat
turn my eyes into mountains
and my heart into the thistle of a rose?
Because for seven years he loved me.
That's all.
And I loved him back.
And with his death he told me:
Sever your connections with the limitations of the self.
Sever your connections with the past.
Then soar into the moment like a Fool.

Sondra and the Big Bones
by Francine M. Storey

1951 was a long time ago — only a heartbeat ago, geologically speaking, but to me, it seems like a long time ago. That's when I was born. May 13, 1951. I was born in the sunny land of sunny California. Now, I suppose that you think that a baby girl born in Hollywood, California should want to be a movie star. That's what my mother thought. She gave me ballet lessons and singing lessons and tap lessons, and she had my picture taken with a giant Hershey bar! She sent me on auditions for movies like *Babes in Toyland*, and I danced the hula at openings of radio stations and grocery stores. There was only one problem: I hated the dancing lessons. I didn't want to be a candy cane or a mouse or a puppet or an elf or even a Sugar Plum Fairy. "What do you want," my mother growled. "I want to be a grown-up girl who digs for the big bones," I whispered. Bones! Yes, bones! The bones of ancient beasts like the ones found at the La Brea Tar Pits, which is right there on La Brea Boulevard near the Farmer's Market and the television studios, but in prehistoric times was a watering hole where camels and tigers and mammoths came to drink and sometimes got stuck in the tar. Yes, I was very sure! Positive! "I want to spend my life digging up mammoth and saber-tooth tiger and camel and even dinosaur bones!" My mother took to her chair. She screamed that I was a weird kid! Who on this entire planet does not want a pair of tap shoes? Only an ungrateful child!

But at last, my stepfather, Red, listened and then every Sunday took me to the Los Angeles County Museum; and there, in the large, large rooms, stood processions of mammoths and dinosaurs. Dinosaurs . . . terrible lizards . . . behemoths almost a block long, teeth the size of a fist! I was happy in the museum. It was dark; it was dusty; it was silent. Sometimes, I stretched up and touched the bones of one of the giants when a guard wasn't looking. I wanted to climb up on top of the dinosaurs and ride them like ladies ride elephants in the circus. I wanted to take the long ride back to the primeval world where the sunrise was green and the sunset was a fiery maroon, where the seas had different shores and jungles grew where icy glaciers now flow. Well, I won the battle, but I didn't win the war. My mother was convinced that I was mentally ill, and honestly, I finally had to give up.

The other day, I took Momma to the Museum of Natural History in New York to see the exhibit of the mosaics from Carthage. She loved the mosaics, but she wouldn't go to the Dinosaur Rooms. I wanted to see the Pterodactyls suspended from the ceiling in a perpetual flight home. I wanted to gape at the prehistoric giant shark's jaw hung across the doorway. Momma didn't even want to see the fossil of the sea serpent from the Badlands of Montana, so I just took her to lunch in the glass-covered restaurant in the Museum, and we were in the midst of a conversation about omelettes when she said to me, "Sondra, you should have become a veterinarian."

A Low Thyroid Case
by Ida Barron

I was always a low thyroid case. Translation: a lazy sleepy-head. It was great; it helped me get away with a lot. Sometimes I put on an act of needing help, but mostly the family just seemed to want to do things for me. Like the time at the dinner table when I reached for my glass of water. My sister's hand got there first. She handed me the glass, waited for me to drink, took the glass, and put it back on the table. My brother-in-law, her husband, watched this. "That's some racket you've got going for you," he said, and laughed. Mama was the worst. She loved to do all my laundry and ironing. In the morning, when I left for work on the run, late as usual, she followed me to the door with freshly squeezed orange juice in hot water. I had to have at least orange juice and something hot to start the day, you understand. On Saturday, when I slept late, she made sure she kept her beloved visiting grandchildren very quiet. Aunt Ida was sleeping. They were quiet, too, though it was hard, since their favorite game was "Tarzan and the Apes." Our living room and all those soft chairs to jump on made a great jungle. When I finally appeared, they greeted me warmly and invited me to join their play. "What part will I take?" I foolishly asked. "You be the elephant," said my favorite nephew. He was immediately demoted to second position. Instead, as a certified low thyroid case, I opted to join my mother, sister and sister-in-law at the kitchen table for coffee, cake and a gossip update. Well, when my doctor, who had been feeding me thyroid pills, pronounced me normal, I was a little sorry. My beautiful alibi was gone!

Feminine
by Chocolate Waters

The word has become hateful.
It reminds you of little girl voices,
clutch purses, ankle bracelets,
clean underwear in case you get hit
by a truck.

Feminine.
The word has lost its woman,
its essence, its puissance,
its delicious smell.
It reminds you of deodorant sprays,
of "female troubles,"
of not enough iron in the diet.

Feminine.
The word has become declassé.
They scorn it in classrooms,
in locker rooms, in gay men.
They scorn it in political matters
and in women's bars.

Feminine.
The word has lost its noblesse,
its butch, butch butchiness.
Feminine.
The word has lost
its balls.

A Special Class
by Ida Barron

I'd like to tell you about my work. I'm a teacher in East Harlem, and I love my job. Here's how my day went today. When I got to my classroom this morning, there was 'Little' Carmen at the door, just standing there.

"She refuses to go in," said the teacher on corridor duty.

"What's wrong, Carmen?" I asked. "Why won't you go in?"

"Day gonna hitch me," she said.

"Come on, you walk in with me. No one will dare hit you."

Actually, that was what Carmen wanted. She brightened up, handed me a tiny American flag for a gift, and went cheerfully to her desk. The flag went on display on the bulletin board.

My class is a multi-grade class of visually handicapped children in an East Harlem elementary school. The children have adjusted surprisingly well to their handicaps and seem to like being in a special class. This morning, some children had already arrived. Others straggled in. Henry hung my coat in the closet. Julia brought me a glass of water. 'Big' Carmen, as usual, came up to inform me about her breakfast. She loves to talk about food. Today she had some "likton" soup. Only Candido, a third-grader, looked uncertain. He was transferred to me yesterday to get him out of the regular third-grade teacher's hair. When I gave the class their individual assignments in arithmetic to start the day, Candido was shocked.

"Again?" he complained. "But I did numbers yesterday."

"Yes, you did. Yesterday, today, tomorrow, again and again, until you know everything. When you hand me a nicely done paper, I'll hang it on the bulletin board."

Frankly, I reinforced this attempt at motivation with a slight poke and added, "Get to work!"

At ten o'clock, we went down to the auditorium for the assembly period, then came back and had our milk and cookies recess. Recess is sometimes perked up with a bit of home-style entertainment. This morning, Elvira asked, "Could I sing that new song we learned in assembly?"

Elvira does not have much of a voice, but she loves to sing, and she loves being "on" and was not in the least self-conscious. The new song was the fourth stanza of *America*. The words, in case you've forgotten, are: "Our Father's God to Thee . . . Author of liberty . . . To Thee we sing. Long may our land be bright . . . With Freedom's holy light . . . Protect us by Thy might . . . Great God, our King."

In Elvira's version, it came out like this: "Ah Fada's Gah tuh dee . . . Awfuh of fliverty . . . Tuh dee we seen. Lawn may ah lan eee bligh . . . Wid Freedon holy fry . . . Puh-tay-ay-tuh-uh ny an my . . . Lay-ay down duh Keeen."

"Elvira," I said, "that's beautiful. Would you sing it again for me? I'd like to write it down!"

Elvira beamed and sang. While Elvira sang, and I wrote, Marvin kept coming up to the basket with bits of paper. He looked over my shoulder nonchalantly each time. Marvin, like the eldest son in the Passover Haggadah, was my wise one. Finally, he couldn't stand it anymore.

"Teacher," he said, "that ain't the way you spell it, the Our Father."

"That's okay," I answered, "I'll fix it up later. Don't worry."

We had a history lesson coming up, so there was no more time for spelling. Since this is a presidential election year and Election Day is nearly here, I thought a discussion about American presidents was in order. Could anyone name one of our great presidents? Peter's hand went up first.

"George Lincoln," he said.

"Well," I said, "that's right, but his first name was Abraham. Abraham Lincoln. However, there was a famous George, and he was famous for something special. Who remembers his name?"

Peter's hand was up first.

"Yes, Peter," I said, trembling slightly.

"That," he said, "was George Washington, and he was Abraham Lincoln's famous father."

Well, we got that straightened out, proceeded to our reading lesson, and then the lunch bell rang. When I got back to the classroom after lunch, I found the class in a bunch up front, instead of in their seats doing the spelling assignment. They were gathered around Nestor and Victoria, with Eugene in the middle. Nestor and Victoria were having a hot argument, back and forth, with Nestor saying, "I know how to hypnotize somebody. I just hypnotized Eugene, and Victoria says I didn't."

And Victoria stood her ground: "Well, you didn't. You're doing it all wrong."

"I did so hypnotize him."

"You did not."

"I did."

"You didn't."

"Tell you what," I interjected, "let's have a demonstration. First Nestor, then Victoria."

Nestor was a golden-haired albino in dark glasses, fairly sure of himself. Victoria, my senior class member, had a lisp, a lively interest in learning new things, and a somewhat bossy style, as befitted her position as class elder. Eugene was a nice, shy boy, the kind that's so easy to overlook, and seemed pleased now to be the center of attention. Nestor stood in front of Eugene and, in a sing-song monotone, repeated, "You're gonna laugh, you're gonna laugh," until the tiniest flicker of a smile crossed Eugene's face.

"See," cried Nestor, "he's hypnotized. I made him laugh."

Victoria haughtily, hands on hips: "That ith not the way to do it."

She stood in front of Eugene, fixed him with a stare, rotated her hands almost in his face and intoned, "You're getting drowthy, you're getting drowthy," until Eugene's eyelids fluttered and his eyes closed for a second.

"Thee, he'th hypnotithed. That'th the right way."

"Well," I said, "you are both very good hypnotists. And now, we'd better get to our spelling." The children sat down, and Eugene did, in fact, have trouble keeping his eyes open!

Thankfully, we were scheduled to go to Central Park to visit the bird sanctuary at one-thirty, a chance for some fresh air. When we got to the park, two characters obviously playing hookey from junior high school approached Nestor. "Uh-oh," I thought, "what do I do if they get tough?" I reached Nestor just as they did.

"Is he Puerto Rican?" they asked. "Could we touch him for luck?" and they proceeded to rub their hands in his golden hair. Then, to my relief, they went on their way.

After our nature lesson in the sanctuary, as we were leaving the park, Marvin, the wise guy, said, "That was great, Teacher. Sanctuary much."

I was so bemused by that, I forgot to be Little Carmen's partner. Back at school, she showed her displeasure.

"Gimme back my flag," she said angrily.

I gave back the flag. The three o'clock bell rang. And that was the end of another day!

My Father

from *Mine on Weekends*

by Roger Cacchiotti

It was an unusually warm day in April. A warm breeze gently brushed against my face as the school bell rang, but my feet were frozen, as if caught in an icy winter storm. My clothes felt so wet and heavy, it was hard to stand up straight. The road home had a gentle slope, but climbing a mountain would have been easier. And along that road home, every lawn was manicured. It sounds strange to say, but each one looked unbearably neat — there was no life.

Would he be there? I wondered. Has he arrived? Has he left? Large bushes, their blossoms barely open, covered the driveway. I turned the corner to my house. His black car was in the driveway. Quickly, I ran to the back door. The house was quiet and still. The smell of ammonia burned my nostrils as I walked into the hallway. Shoes were neatly arranged in a row along the hallway wall. The kitchen was spotless, with every last dish in its place. Unbearably neat.

Walking into the front hallway, I heard him upstairs in the bedroom. I ran up the stairs two at a time. Turning the corner into the bedroom, I saw him. He stood by the closet, removing his clothes from the rod, his white undershirt exposing his lean, muscular body, his baggy pants keeping the rest of his form a secret. Slicked back and perfectly groomed, his hair accented his high cheekbones and chiseled face. A lit cigarette hung from his mouth, the smoke forcing him to squint his eyes. Without a word, he gazed through me, neatly placing his shirts into his suitcase on the bed.

He forcefully inhaled a long drag from his cigarette, blowing it out with one long puff. Turning to me, my father said, "The bitch has thrown me out." Leaning against the wall, tears soaking my face, I said, "I love you, I'll always love you no matter what happens." With his back facing me, he said, "Thank you," grabbing another armful of clothes.

"Please hug me, please hold me," I cried to myself, remembering his strong arms embracing me. "Please hold me like you used to." But he kept packing his bags. Sitting on my knees, I watched as he walked past me with his closed bag.

Each stair creaked as he walked down to the living room. I trailed closely behind him, trying to catch the familiar scent of his cologne. He got down on one knee and started packing books from the living room bookshelf. Handing me John F. Kennedy's *Profiles in Courage*, he said, "If you only read one more book, make it this one." Clutching it tightly, I knew I would never read a page.

He got up, closed the box, and put the suitcase strap over his shoulder. He picked up the box and walked out the back door to the car. He put the suitcase and box into the trunk. Then he got into the car, slamming the door as he started the engine. As I rushed to the driveway, I barely caught a glimpse of his car speeding down the road. Underneath the grapevines, behind the garage, I lay down crying, praying I would fall asleep. That was the last time I ever saw him.

I Believed in Dreams Then
by David A. Green

I was so young then, so naive. I still believed in my dreams. I believed, I felt so strongly, that I could make a real difference. I was eager to go to Africa with the Peace Corps and alter the course of human history in two years! Go out there and change centuries of injustice and monstrous cruelty with the sheer force of will and my bare hands. Why did I feel this way? Because of you, of course. I was desperately in love with you. I'm not sure you ever understood. It was the kind of love that is all-consuming, and at the same time gives this feeling of "I can do anything!" And after you left, that first sun-drenched morning, you didn't know it, but I saw you skipping . . . skipping down the alley — the image of happiness! And as I watched you, I was still trembling from new feelings I didn't quite know how to define. And then it all stopped, as though someone had slammed a door so hard that the ringing in my ears was shattering. Why? Why did it stop? Did I suddenly become that unappealing? And where did you go? On to a new conquest, someone equally naive? Where did you go? Where are you now? Will I ever be able to get you out of my head?

The Banker and the Teddy Bear
by Mark Wellen

I was catching up on some reading last night, and in the newspaper I came across an article written by a banker in Santa Barbara, California. He had gone to his office on a Saturday morning and, as he opened the curtains, frightened away a homeless man sleeping in the bushes against the side of the building, directly underneath his window. After the man took off, the banker couldn't stop thinking about him and went outside. As he was looking at the place in the bushes where the man had slept, the banker discovered that in the man's haste to leave, he had left behind a weathered, fading teddy bear, with eyes that didn't match, one just a white button, most of the fur worn, stuffing coming out under one arm. And there it sat, leaning a little to the right . . . alone. As I read this, I felt as the banker felt, and tears came to my eyes. It touched me. I also felt as the homeless man must have felt, leaving behind his one and only friend. But what I felt most was . . . was that I was like the teddy bear — alone, waiting for someone to come and find me . . . and take me . . . gently . . . and give me a long . . . slow . . . rocking hug.

Blondes
by Jim Shewalter

I had a dream last night. You were in it. Did you ever see the movie, *The Time Machine?* The one where Rod Taylor rides into the future on a sled with a big whirling disk on the back. Anyway, it doesn't matter. When Rod Taylor gets to the future, it's all blondes running and frolicking by the water. He can't believe how beautiful it is. He meets this girl named, are you ready, Weena. The whole movie's too Freudian for me. Anyway, in the film, Weena is showing Rod around and vapidly being blonde, when suddenly out of nowhere, these horns go off, and the blondes walk like zombies into a cave. Later in the movie, we find out that the blondes are being eaten by Morlocks. They're these big, ugly, green monsters. This is where you come in. Just kidding. Anyway, the Morlocks' dietary plan is offensive to most audiences, so Rod Taylor decides to infiltrate their underground home and save Weena. After a great struggle, all is set right; the blondes are released to frolic and the Morlocks are deprived dinner. This is, after all, a Hollywood film and a cautionary tale. The subliminal message: never eat anything cute.

Anyway, my dream, I started all this to tell you my dream. In the dream, I'm sitting on exhibit somewhere. I'm staring out at an audience that is slowly turning blonde. Not all at once, but slowly, one at a time. It's clear time is passing, but the audience doesn't change. They just keep turning blonde. Then the horns go off. Only no one gets up. I hear the horns as well, but all I do is sit there. I can tell something destructive is happening outside. I sense malice all around me, and it scares me to death. I want to leave, but I don't dare get up. Suddenly, my chair becomes the time machine. I pull the control backward, and the scene changes. I'm going back in time. The years keep rolling back. Before I know it, I'm back at home watching TV. You're there, Mother and Dad are there, and we all keep getting younger. Mother and Dad are now in their twenties. It's real strange to see the two of them looking so young. You become a tiny baby, then disappear. I have to stop the time machine, or I'll disappear like you did. Mother and Dad are talking. I'm just a baby, but I know they're fighting. Fighting about me and I can't defend myself. I feel the need to get the hell out of there, so I push the control forward until I hear the horns again. I stop the machine. The blondes are still watching me. That's when I woke up. Are you still with me? Don't give me that look. I'm just trying to tell you I've decided not to move to California.

Overnight Train
by Peter DeMarco

When I was ten years old, we took an overnight train trip to Florida. It was my first real vacation out among other people. Usually we went somewhere in the car, and so it was just us. But this time, we went Amtrak. And I had the window seat. Mom sat with Dad, Aunt Marie sat with Uncle Charlie, and my brother Paul and sister Linda sat together. That left me and an empty seat. I felt left out, and I remember thinking, "Why do I have to be the one to sit next to some stranger?" My seat mate turned out to be a middle-aged black woman, very maternal-looking, wearing a little hat and a gray wool coat. As the train started to move very, very slowly, she put her arm around me and waved goodbye through the train window to her husband, who was standing on the platform. "He's with me," she said, very proudly. I had never been that close to a black person before. I felt awkward. During the night, Uncle Charlie woke us all up, yelling to the conductor that there was no heat. He kept repeating, "My wife is freezing!" I could hear him, but from a distance — you know how it is when you're in a deep sleep. But then I felt something covering me, and I opened my eyes just enough to see the woman wrapping her coat around me, and I felt so cared for! I awoke the next morning. It was very early, and the coat was still on me. I took it off, put it on the empty seat beside me — the woman was not there — and I tried to brush some intangible thing from myself. The thought of having a black person's coat on me made me uncomfortable. Then the woman returned and sat down, holding the folded coat on her lap. She leaned over and told my parents that she took care of me. I felt ashamed.

I Tested Positive
Anonymous

I'm sorry to tell you that I have AIDS. I had taken the test in 1985, and it was negative, so I was very surprised when I got sick last year. I found out just before Christmas. But, I have been very lucky. I started taking the few drugs that are available and gained back the weight I lost. Except for a nasty allergic reaction to one of my medications, I feel good most of the time, and people tell me I look fine.

Of course, having AIDS has changed my life. I stopped working. To supplement what I get from disability insurance, I'm using up most of the money in my savings account. What was I saving it for, a rainy day? In many ways, my life is going better than before my diagnosis, although it is at great cost. I am clearer about what I want. My relationships are closer. I seldom do anything I don't want to do. Why should I? What are they going to do, kill me? I understand the phrase "living in the moment" in a way I never did before, especially in the middle of the night when I get scared and have to remind myself that I am healthy now and worrying about the future doesn't accomplish anything. As a matter of fact, except for the fact that dealing with chronic life-threatening illness stinks, I'm glad for the changes that have occurred.

I don't want you to think that I am going to drop dead tomorrow, although the statistics say that I probably will die before there is a cure. So far, I am doing great, except for occasional bouts of despair, anger, sadness and/or fear as I try to deal with the prospect of becoming ill. I try to remember that there are always exceptions to statistics.

I hope I am the first person you know with AIDS.

Job Satisfaction
by Jon Wool

Next time you're near a cop, take a look at his hands. You ever see these guys' hands? Big, thick, chunky, beefy hands. Masculine hands. Macho hands. Notice the little scars, nicks and cuts on the back, hard, round callouses on the front, swollen joints and knuckles. We're talking about hands that have been there and back again. Hands that don't gotta prove nothing to nobody. Now look at my hands. Long, thin, sensitive hands. Delicate hands. Sissy hands. Faggot hands. I've always had a problem with my masculinity. When I joined the Force, I became so caught up with this sense of macho bullshit that I couldn't even see straight. I learned to walk macho, talk macho, eat, drink, sleep macho. I even learned to breathe macho. A macho cop isn't a good cop. He's a bad cop. A dumb cop. A couple of nights ago, my partner and I were on a routine call. Couple of kids had run out on a check in a fancy restaurant. My partner goes around front, I go around back. I find this guy hiding behind some garbage pails. I know it's the perpetrator because of the way he's dressed and because there's no one else around. I walk up to him and I say, "Alright, buddy. On your feet!" The guy stands up, looks me in the eye and says, "Fuck you. Fuck you." I say, "NO! Fuck you!" And with that, I hit him. I took my night stick, I swung, I connected, I followed through. You couldn't have hit a better home run than I did. And suddenly, I felt great. I felt fantastic. Better than I had in years. I mean, I didn't hurt the guy badly or anything. But all that pressure. All that aggravation just seemed to disappear. And I thought to myself, "This job is very, very therapeutic."

Let Me Tell You One Thing
by James Miller

Let me tell you one thing. You ask how I am? I'll tell you how I am. I'm tired. Yes, I'm tired. I'm tired of having to be pleasant. I'm tired of having to always look nice so as not to be confused with a mugger. I'm tired of hidden agendas where you think you have a job and you don't. I'm tired of having to look acceptable in better stores so as not to be eyed suspiciously and treated like a shoplifter. I'm tired of having to prove innocence so as not to be presumed guilty. I'm tired of having to ask directions, or for the time, at a safe distance of four feet or more so as not to instill fear of attack. I'm tired of being dismissed as having a bad day when I've had a bad decade. I'm tired of the news media telling the world that no one, and I mean not a living ass, commits violent or drug-related crimes in this goddamn country except black people. I'm tired of being angry. I'm tired of wanting . . . striving . . . talking loud and saying nothing . . . listening but not hearing anything . . . seeking and not finding a goddamn thing but bullshit. Oh, and one more thing . . . I'm tired of you. I'm outta here.

Turn It Around
by Kurt Sproul

This whole thing started just a year ago or so, when I wound up in the hospital, pretty banged up from some idiot running a red light. I was able to move around after four or five days. My family lives out of state and had to get back to their business after they saw I'd be okay, and I didn't have many friends since I had recently relocated. The truth is, I guess I was pretty lonesome.

One of the nurses suggested I try visiting other patients during my little hobbles up and down the hall. This was pretty helpful for me and for the others, too. As I was able to walk further, the nurse asked if I'd like to visit the AIDS patients. I told her I didn't think so, and that gays weren't my favorite people . . . that's a whole 'nother story. But then, I figured they wouldn't all be gay there anyway; anyone can get AIDS, right?

The first guy I became friends with was Greg, a real nice guy I never would have guessed was gay. You wouldn't even be able to tell that he was sick, except he was pretty skinny and had a lot of tubes going into him. I'd go in to see him every day during the weeks I was there. But then I got sent home. After that we would speak on the phone. A couple of months went by, and I was able to drive again, so I went back to see him. He was lying in bed with his legs uncovered, up on pillows. They were burned beyond belief. He explained it was skin cancer, and they'd been trying to treat it with radiation and chemotherapy. He'd gotten burned really bad from the radiation.

But there was something worse, which he couldn't understand. His friends had stopped calling, stopped visiting. That seemed to be the hardest thing for him to take. The doctors had told him they had done all they could and were sending him home. But his roommate wanted him to find somewhere else to live. I found myself saying things I can't talk about right now . . . about why his friends weren't around. I could only explain why I was there, trying to make up for not being there for my good friend Bobby when he needed me a few years back. See, Bobby had Kaposi. He was covered with purple sores, and he was in and out of consciousness. Every time I'd try to leave, he'd come to and beg me to stay. I felt trapped and scared. Once I even broke down in the parking lot. I decided I couldn't go back to see him again. I guess that's what I'm trying to turn around.

Short Time
by David M. Mead

I was short time. Ten days. They should have pulled me off the line. They should have pulled us all off the line. We were ready to go home. Been looking forward to it. Fuck, we were living for it. Going home. Home to Sunday football and cheerleaders in short-short skirts. Home to blood-red steaks and round-eyed women. Home to the world.

There was this one guy in our unit. Stupid son-of-a-bitch. He didn't want to leave. He liked the Nam. Shit, he loved the Nam. Stoking slants and hosing villages. He used to get out of his vehicle, stand on the top and cheer when incoming rounds were firing. He had turned really weird. So all-American clean he squeaked when he did boom-boom with some slope whore. He went bad real fast. Well, not bad. Just nasty. Yeah, nasty. Could have been bad. But Sarg was there. Sarg wouldn't let anybody go bad. Kept us straight. As straight as you could be in the Nam.

This kid . . . Sarg loved him. Watched over this kid. We thought they were queer for each other. Shit, why not. Might as well fuck a guy you love than a cunt you have to pay. Boom-boom. Boom-boom. *(In dialect.)* Hey, G.I. boy, yo make boom-boom with me, cost you ten dolla. Don't be dinki-duo. Spend ten dolla. Me no give you drippy dick. *(As the sergeant.)* Soldier boy, don't go wasting your money in no God-damn Gook titty bar. Down the street is some nice Philippino pussy. Get your rocks off there. *(Himself.)* Yeah, getting a piece in the Nam. Getting stoned in the Nam.

Just don't get wasted in the Nam. Waste them, man. Waste the little yellow bastards. Watch that flank. Don't stand up when the flares go off. Get down, motherfucker, get down. Cong in the wire; Cong in the wire. Shoot the bastard, shithead. Going home, sir. I am home. Where? New Jersey. Where the fuck is that? We're short time. Ten days. We'll be home for Christmas. I ain't shitting you, Doug. Don't look at me like that. I ain't weirded out. What are you? On the rag? You're fucking with my head, Doug. I'm not watching where we're going . . . Don't die. Don't die. Don't die on me, Doug. Please don't die . . .

Dr. and Mrs. Mitchell, the Government of the United States and the Department of Defense is pleased to inform you that your son, Corporal Daniel Mitchell, will be honorably discharged from the United States Army at Lyons Military Hospital on December 2, 1972, and assigned to the outpatient program of the Veteran's Administration. We are happy to report that he has made a full recovery from his wounds and is to be awarded a Purple Heart in addition to the Bronze Star awarded in May 1971. The United States is very proud of Corporal Daniel Mitchell, as you must be. Signed Richard Milhouse Nixon, President of the United States.

What the fuck do I do now?

One Handed
by Garrison Phillips

There's a snapshot in the album back home of my
Dad holding me one-handed, high over his head, when I
was about two years old. His left arm is straight up,
and I'm perched there, smart aleck-like, with this goofy
grin on my face. My Dad had lost his right arm in an
accident when he was just 12 years old. The double-
barreled shotgun had a broken trigger guard, and he
had been shooting at a fox from on top of the chicken
house. The trigger caught on the roof edge of the
chicken house as he leaned over to hand the gun to his
father and — BAM — the other barrel went off smack
into his armpit. But he never complained about that
loss. No one ever heard him say "what if" or "help me."
He just relearned to do everything left handed and plain
set out and did whatever had to be done.

One night just after I had arrived in Korea, I had
been sent out a few hundred yards in front of the line to
pick up extra equipment dropped by a patrol on their
way out earlier that evening — extra ammo, commo
wire, a light machine gun — and on my way back, all of
a sudden, I knew that the enemy was infiltrating our
lines. It was more than that creepy feeling when you
know someone is behind you, because I could smell
them. The onions and garlic they cooked with their rice
rations was so strong. I lit out straight up the slope
towards our line and just went right up and over our
sandbags. I had my M-1 and ammo bandoliers slung
over my shoulder, commo wire around my neck, and the
light machine gun in my left hand, and I just went
straight up and over that 12-foot wall. The guys in my
platoon couldn't figure out how I did it, all loaded down
like that. Later that night, when I had time to think
about it, I seemed to remember feeling my Dad's hand

pushing me up and over the sandbags. He had died real sudden of cancer when I was in the final week of basic training just a month before, and he was still on my mind a lot. Or maybe it's true — you know, that the soul hangs around for awhile in this world until it crosses over or whatever. Maybe my Dad hung around to look after me for awhile. Anyway, that's how I like to think about it.

Grandmothers
by John Dunne

They are out of place now, but that doesn't mean that they're leaving. Their escape route has been cut off for years. Their children plead with them to get out, but they have stayed too long at the fair. They are the grandmothers, and they are our treasure, a treasure that will soon be gone and fondly remembered, like the trolley cars they once dodged with their baby carriages, in and out of the traffic on Fordham Road. Today, they lean on canes and walkers instead of carriages, and they dodge bicycles instead of trolleys. Shopping bags and pocketbooks hang from arthritic hands, empty except for a few dollars of "mugging money." Their real money is pinned to their underwear, just enough to pay for what they will need that day. Their charge cards and jewelry are home, hidden in bed linen and upholstery, protected by locks and chains and steel bars.

They are the moving targets in the arcade, armed only with rosary beads and determination. They are a cooperative of so-called "seniors," organized to travel together whenever they do brave the streets, and to telephone one another each morning to make sure that the membership is intact. You never see them at night, because they are home before dark, hostages in their own homes.

Despite all the advantages they gave us, we didn't do as well as they did — in staying married, in raising children, in managing their lives. They accomplished so much more after starting with so little: no college courses in how to grow old with dignity, no pop psychology books on how to raise a lot of good children through a lot of bad times. And they stay informed. They read newspapers, even if it is not all the news that's fit to print. They keep alert, even if it is in front of a television set. And they stimulate their minds, listening to voices, not music, on the radio, their oldest and dearest friend. They always vote, never come to your home without bringing a thoughtful gift, and whatever they are dressed in, it is clean, ironed and appropriate.

Their children return to the neighborhood to visit them, some on a regular basis, some only once a year at Christmas or Thanksgiving. "You come to us," they say. "It will be a nice change of scenery for you." What they really mean is that mother's scenery would not be a nice change for them!

To be fair, it is not always easy doing business with the grandmothers. They can remember what earrings they wore to a wedding fifty years ago, but cannot remember where they left their pocketbooks five minutes ago. They never so much as polished a car, never mind drove one, but that doesn't stop them from informing you that "we are going to be late," "we are never going to get there," or "we never should have gone in the first place." You have raised a child of your own, survived two years in the military, been appointed an officer of your firm, but they can make you feel like you are still going through potty training. Often they convey these messages without uttering a sound. You gather all your good news to cheer them up, but the grandmothers have been playing "ain't it awful" that day, and your good news doesn't stand a chance.

But they raise your children when your marriage doesn't take, offer you their savings when you find yourself out of work, and tell you the truth when others tell you what they think you want to hear. These are our grandmothers — our treasures.

Scenes

Daisy & Esmond
from *The Vocal Lesson & Two*

by Gabriel Walsh

ESMOND. Daisy?

DAISY. My car's parked near a driveway. I can't stay long. I couldn't resist stopping to say hello.

ESMOND. I'm glad to see you.

DAISY. I parked near a driveway. I hope I'm not blocking anyone. I didn't interrupt you, did I?

ESMOND. No.

DAISY. Are you having coffee?

ESMOND. Yeah.

DAISY. God, it's impossible.

ESMOND. What?

DAISY. I'm telling you, it's impossible. You can go about searching and looking all you want to, but that's not it. You know, I really have had it with all those people I used to know. I'm so glad to have found an individual who is his own man and who doesn't care about that flashy way of life. It's impossible going about like that every day of your life. You know, they're never satisfied. You know what I'm talking about.

ESMOND. I'm a little confused. What? What's impossible?

DAISY. Oh, come on . . .

ESMOND. What time is it?

DAISY. Close to seven. I parked near a driveway. I hope I'm not blocking anyone. You know, getting along with another person doesn't have to be all that complicated. It's impossible the way it was.

ESMOND. What's impossible?

DAISY. We haven't seen each other for some time, am I right?

ESMOND. Yeah, it's been a while. Would you like a cup of coffee?

DAISY. Yeah, sure, why not. I guess my car's okay. So I get a ticket, so what.

ESMOND. What's impossible?

DAISY. What's impossible? Oh, God! I came by to tell you that I've finally met the right person. He's absolutely fantastic! You know, it's just like I always said. You've just got to be yourself. You always find out in the end that it is best to wait. You know what I'm talking about.

ESMOND. You're getting married?

DAISY. It's true.

ESMOND. Who is he?

DAISY. He's a lawyer. He's really special.

ESMOND. You take cream and sugar?

DAISY. Of course! You know that.

ESMOND. Well, you might have changed since we went around together. So, tell me, where did you meet him? What's he like?

DAISY. Oh, well, I don't know what to say. He's just not like others I've gone out with. He's simple and basic. His head is in the right place, thank God. You know, I'm glad I went out of town. I was getting absolutely fed up. Meeting the same faces every day. Everybody with the same thing to say. I'm telling you, it was a bloody bore. Every morning was just . . . I'm telling you it was just ridiculous! I couldn't stand it.

ESMOND. You went out of town?

DAISY. Yes. Didn't I say that?

ESMOND. Well, I guess you did. I'm sorry, I got wrapped up in looking at you.

DAISY. What?

ESMOND. It's true. You've changed.

DAISY. Well, thank God!

ESMOND. You still have that smile.

DAISY. My smile?

ESMOND. Yes. It's got a lot behind it.

DAISY. Why, thank you. Oh God, I hope I don't get a

ticket. I'm parked in the driveway, or next to one, whatever.

ESMOND. You still have the same car?

DAISY. Of course! I love it. I absolutely adore that car. It's a marvelous car.

ESMOND. So now you have a lawyer.

DAISY. Well, he's a man with an absolutely marvelous attitude. It's just a pleasure to . . .

ESMOND. Not like mine, eh?

DAISY. Oh, well, you're you. I mean, it doesn't matter, really. I understand you. You have your own particular way in life. I know you.

ESMOND. Oh, yeah?

DAISY. Well, never mind that. You've a perfect right to be the way you are. I'm not being critical.

ESMOND. Hmmm . . . I'm happy to see you. You look good.

DAISY. Thank you. I feel good. I really do.

ESMOND. That's a nice hat.

DAISY. Thank you. How are things with you?

ESMOND. The same.

DAISY. The same?

ESMOND. Yeah.

DAISY. Oh, come on.

ESMOND. It's true.

DAISY. Really?

ESMOND. Yeah. That's a very nice dress you've got on.

DAISY. Thank you.

ESMOND. Have you set a date yet?

DAISY. Almost.

ESMOND. And he's a lawyer?

DAISY. Yes.

ESMOND. How old?

DAISY. Two years older than I am. I'm telling you, he's fantastic.

ESMOND. Different from your usual type.

44

DAISY. My usual type? What do you mean?

ESMOND. Well, you used to go out with singers, painters . . . you know, the artistic types.

DAISY. God, don't remind me. I'm tired of starving artists. Actually, Esmond, you and Cliff are similar.

ESMOND. Cliff?

DAISY. Cliff! Yes! That's his name.

ESMOND. The man you're getting married to?

DAISY. Yes, Cliff!

ESMOND. What about him?

DAISY. I said you are similar. You both have similar qualities.

ESMOND. We do?

DAISY. It's interesting. It really is.

ESMOND. Have you lost weight?

DAISY. No!

ESMOND. Well, you look like you have.

DAISY. Cliff even looks a bit like you, or the way you'd look in a shirt and tie.

ESMOND. I see you're letting your hair grow.

DAISY. Yes.

ESMOND. It looks good.

DAISY. Thank you.

ESMOND. You really look like you've lost weight, Daisy.

DAISY. You're kidding me.

ESMOND. I'm not.

DAISY. That's incredible. Cliff and I have been going out every night. Spanish restaurants, Italian places. You name it, I've been eating it.

ESMOND. It doesn't show. Could I see that hat for a second? *(Daisy hands him the hat.)* I like this hat. What's that?

DAISY. What?

ESMOND. That cloth that's wrapped around you.

DAISY. Oh, that's a belt.

ESMOND. Could I look at it? *(She takes off her belt*

and hands it to him.) Interesting material.

DAISY. Cliff bought it. It's from South America.

ESMOND. No kidding.

DAISY. He goes down there on business sometimes.

ESMOND. South America?

DAISY. Yes.

ESMOND. You've got good taste.

DAISY. He picked it out.

ESMOND. Here, sit down.

DAISY. I hope my car isn't blocking anybody's way out there.

ESMOND. The worst you can get is a ticket.

DAISY. Or be towed away. *(They sit down together on the bed.)*

ESMOND. Your hair really looks good this way. *(After a beat, he reaches to her feet and takes her shoes off.)* I love your feet, Daisy. Beautiful originals. You look like you've been doing a lot of exercise since I've been around you. *(He leans over and kisses her. She then puts her arms around him, and they embrace fully. Esmond reaches out and turns off the lamp next to the bed.)* Daisy, when did you say you were getting married? *(They embrace in the dark.)*

Etienne & Simone
from *Vampire Dawn*
by Dennis Horvitz

SIMONE. You killed Martine.

ETIENNE. Yes.

SIMONE. Etienne, she . . . she . . .

ETIENNE. She made you a vampire.

SIMONE. How did you know?

ETIENNE. Your footfall. Vampires move differently than mortals do. Your body isn't completely dead yet, and you already move like a vampire. I could hear your footsteps long before you came into the room.

SIMONE. This feeling! I've never experienced the night this way before! I can hear conversations on the street just by concentrating. The colors, the smells. Is this death?

ETIENNE. This is living death.

SIMONE. Etienne, why did Martine choose me?

ETIENNE. For two reasons. The first and most important, because she's a killer. Just like me. And now, just like you.

SIMONE. And the second?

ETIENNE. To get at me. She knew that I cared about you as a mortal. She knew that I would do anything to protect you. In her jealousy, she has chosen the one act that would hurt me. She knew that I could not bear the idea of you roaming the night, an unclean thing, needing to kill.

SIMONE. But Etienne! This sensation! This power! I think I'm beginning to understand.

ETIENNE. You haven't killed yet. If you haven't killed, you don't understand.

SIMONE. But why must I kill people? Couldn't I live off of animals?

ETIENNE. You could, but for how long? What will

you do when you've finally cleared the area of every rat and stray dog or cat? What will you do when the need becomes so intense that even the simplest motion is agony? I have seen vampires die of hunger, Simone. Your wildest imagination cannot conceive the sight — or the screams.

SIMONE. But I don't feel like killing.

ETIENNE. That is because Martine fed you as she made you. By this time tomorrow, you will do what you will be driven to do until the end of time.

SIMONE. Is there no hope?

ETIENNE. *(He takes her hand.)* Hmmm . . . a very human gesture, really. A symbol of communication, of comfort, of strength. Yes, there is hope, because after all this time, I finally have the courage.

SIMONE. Courage for what, Etienne?

ETIENNE. To do what must be done.

SIMONE. What do you mean? What must be done?

ETIENNE. The first step is, we wait.

SIMONE. Wait for what?

ETIENNE. We wait for the sunrise.

Jane & Roger
from *The Prism*
by Dennis Sook

JANE. The doctor said we could stay here in the chapel and talk.

ROGER. Okay, sure.

JANE. Oh, God. What are we going to do?

ROGER. I don't know. It's not fair. None of it. That poor little thing. It has a heart, and it is beating. How can that be? How can it have such a tiny, healthy heart and everything else be so . . .

JANE. Maybe it's something we don't understand.

ROGER. We understand it well enough. It is what it is. It's got multiple birth defects. That's what the doctor said.

JANE. Please don't call her "it." She has a name. Melanie. She is a human being. She's alive, and she belongs to you and me.

ROGER. That's not true. She doesn't belong to me. Nor to you either. She's no part of us. Just what do you suppose those doctors can do with surgery? Make her a whole person from assorted parts? You're mistaken if you think that. They can't do a damn thing.

JANE. The doctor said the decision must be made now. Oh, God.

ROGER. "Oh, God" is right. You're the one that believes in that. Well, what does your God tell you to do?

JANE. To keep her alive and to care for her forever.

ROGER. It's been seven days today. Seems appropriate to me that on the seventh day, your God rested. So, today he's resting. Resting where? Gone fishing? Out to lunch, back in an hour? Get the bastard here, because I want to talk to Him. Now.

JANE. Don't. Don't talk like that. It's not God's fault.

ROGER. Then whose fault is it?

JANE. We don't know why these things happen.

ROGER. Whose fault is it? Mine? Yours?

JANE. It's not anybody's fault.

ROGER. I don't accept that.

JANE. Please.

ROGER. Maybe we shouldn't have used birth control pills. Maybe you shouldn't have experimented with drugs back in your college days.

JANE. What?

ROGER. You heard me.

JANE. Are you blaming me? Are you saying this is my fault? You took drugs, too, back then. Maybe it's your fault.

ROGER. I need to know why our baby was born like this.

JANE. It's God's will. We must accept that. She is a special baby. There are special schools . . .

ROGER. No, no, no, it's a mistake. Honest to Christ, they gave us the wrong one. I can't deal with this. I'm serious. I cannot handle this for the rest of my life. I refuse to be responsible for it, and nobody can make me.

JANE. But we are responsible for Melanie. We're all she has, and we are going to tell the doctor to do the operation. To do everything in his power to give her the best possible chance in the world.

ROGER. Chance? What chance does it have? Chance for what? No, no, no, we are not going to.

JANE. We have to.

ROGER. We don't have to. And we won't. It isn't fair to it . . . her.

JANE. She didn't ask to be born; we wanted her. I love her. I don't care what you say, she has as much right to live as you do, and we'll tell the doctor to do whatever he can.

ROGER. No, we won't. If I have to, I'll . . . I will stop

her living myself. And damn you.

JANE. No, you won't. You couldn't do that. God will give us the strength we need to . . .

ROGER. I've heard all I want to hear about your absentee God. It doesn't exist.

JANE. Stop it. Stop it. Stop it. God is that sweet little baby. God is you and me and our blessed little girl. Please, please, please. Let them help her.

ROGER. It'll be alright. It'll be alright. I promise you. I promise. Alright. It will be alright. We'll talk to the doctor again. Just please, don't cry anymore.

Martha & Joycie
Anonymous

JOYCIE. I brought you a little present.

MARTHA. Is it a peace offering or a bribe?

JOYCIE. It's been a long three years. Will you take it?

MARTHA. I'm not sure what to do. How about a brandy?

JOYCIE. Sure. How's Spencer? I mean, Billie told me you had a boyfriend named Spencer.

MARTHA. That brother of mine does have a mouth. In any case, I'm not seeing Spencer anymore. You wouldn't have liked him. He's too domineering.

JOYCIE. I like domineering men. As long as they're young and use their tongues a lot.

MARTHA. Really?

JOYCIE. Oh, don't get me wrong. I don't want to get married to them. Nobody's taking me on that trip again. But sex, that's another thing. And I do like the young, strong, silent type.

MARTHA. I . . . You've changed . . . I . . .

JOYCIE. I always liked domineering men. That was the problem . . . oh, you mean the sex thing. Yeah, I've changed. It started in the first place I was in, that place where I got the shock treatments that was like a country club. I was the only adult in the place, really. Everybody else was a teenager from some rich family trying to get off drugs or get rid of their schizophrenia. All the young girls there went braless.

MARTHA. So, you started doing it?

JOYCIE. Why not? Still don't wear one. Why give up a good thing?

MARTHA. I suppose . . .

JOYCIE. I had an affair with one of the boys there. He was really mature for his age, really charismatic, kind of like a Michael J. Fox, you know, in the movie where he almost fell in love with his own mother?

MARTHA. You had an affair with a teenager?

JOYCIE. He taught me a lot.

MARTHA. You don't say.

JOYCIE. He made me feel wonderful. You know sex was never any great shakes with me and your father. And then after your dad and I divorced . . . it had been so long since I'd experienced . . .

MARTHA. Do we have to get into this? I don't think I'm ready for this discussion.

JOYCIE. I didn't mean to embarrass you. It's just that a lot has happened to me since my breakdown. Of course, those treatments patched me right up. I'm as good as new now.

MARTHA. Are you really . . . okay? What do the doctors say?

JOYCIE. They say I'm A-number one, made of the right stuff, as long as I keep taking my lithium. I was a very sick woman, Martha, I know that. I'm sure that I caused you and your brother a lot of pain. I said things, and the way I was acting . . .

MARTHA. It's over now. You just said you're cured. Alright?

JOYCIE. I didn't mean to have a breakdown, Martha. It just happened. One day I was in the car, and I got this urge to drive right into a tree.

MARTHA. You did.

JOYCIE. Only I didn't manage to kill myself. But after that day, it was as if I was a balloon that somebody had let go of. I was floating so far away. Have you ever felt that way?

MARTHA. No, and I certainly don't ever want to.

JOYCIE. I'm talking too much about myself. What about you?

MARTHA. What about me?

JOYCIE. You and Reggie got divorced, and now this

new boyfriend Spencer hasn't worked out.

MARTHA. I'm not dwelling on it.

JOYCIE. Guess it's no wonder. Those kinds of things run in families. I divorced your father.

MARTHA. Don't say that! I'm nothing like you, understand? Nothing!

JOYCIE. Sure, sweetheart, I know. You're much smarter than I am, Martha, always have been. And much prettier . . . and nicer.

MARTHA. I'm not that nice . . . wasn't that nice to you when you had your breakdown. I just couldn't . . .

JOYCIE. You were right there with me, Martha, all the way. So was Billie.

MARTHA. Mom, I stopped visiting.

JOYCIE. Yes, after a while.

MARTHA. It was so confusing. So deeply disturbing, to see you change.

JOYCIE. I'm sorry.

MARTHA. Don't you see, I feel guilty. You're my own mother, and when you had a nervous breakdown, I just ran out on you. I couldn't do anything. My father was a helpless alcoholic, and I couldn't do anything for him either.

JOYCIE. How could you? You were a kid.

MARTHA. I tried, though. When I was a teenager, I used to look for him on the streets. I heard you say on the phone to Aunt Carolyn that he'd gone down so far that he was hanging out drunk on street corners.

JOYCIE. Poor Martha, I didn't mean for you to hear that. It was only for a while that your dad was that bad off.

MARTHA. Don't try to whitewash things. I know how far down he was, otherwise he would have come to see me and Billie. He didn't come to see us because he was ashamed. I only figured that out later.

JOYCIE. He didn't come to see you because I wouldn't let him.

MARTHA. How could you stop him?

JOYCIE. I had a court order. He used to beat me up, remember?

MARTHA. He wouldn't have let a court order stop him. I'm sorry for the way he treated you, but my father loved me. He would have gone through anything to be with me. The reason he stopped visiting is because he was ashamed.

JOYCIE. That was part of it, I'm sure.

MARTHA. Don't you see, I'm the dilemma?

JOYCIE. About Dad?

MARTHA. No. About what I'm doing with my life. If I don't do something for somebody before I die, I'll consider myself an A-number one failure. Of course, as a social worker, I was a flop.

JOYCIE. But you're doing great as a consultant, right? What do you consult people in, again?

MARTHA. Image. I just got some new video equipment. I'm working for this company right now. But I'd like to have my own business. I'm good at it. Of course, I can't say it's very altruistic. I do make lots of money, though.

JOYCIE. Nothing wrong with that. And I'm sure that the people you work with appreciate whatever it is you're giving them. What do you do? Tell them how to dress?

MARTHA. Among other things.

JOYCIE. What about me? Think I could use an image consultant?

MARTHA. I wouldn't know where to begin.

JOYCIE. We're nothing alike, are we? You're so smart-looking, and I'm . . . guess no one would ever know we're mother and daughter.

MARTHA. I think I look something like you.

JOYCIE. Come on . . .

MARTHA. You were so beautiful when I was . . .

JOYCIE. And now I'm a mess.

MARTHA. I didn't say that.

JOYCIE. We may not look like mother and daughter, but I still feel like we are. How do you feel?

MARTHA. The same way, I guess, but so much has happened. There's nothing to hold on to.

JOYCIE. All the same, I love you, Martha. Guess I'll go. Thanks for seeing me. I just wanted to make sure you were okay and let you see I'm still in one piece in spite of everything.

MARTHA. I'd . . . I'd like to see you again, sometime.

JOYCIE. Yeah? Well, I'll give you my telephone number. I've got this little apartment. Still needs to be fixed up. You'll have to give me a few weeks to have you over. It's messy.

MARTHA. It's okay if it's messy . . . Mom. See you soon, I hope. Oh, thanks for the present.

JOYCIE. You bet, sweetie.

Margo & Sulynn
from *Bloomin', A Novel in Three Acts*
by Maria Ciaccia

MARGO. Okay, I'm here. So what did you find out?

SULYNN. I'm going to tell you everything I know. I did some nosing around, phone calls and stuff, like when I was a corporate spy. Lars was fired from his position at the hospital, but I can't find out why. Whatever it is, he's not able to get another job as a doctor, so he can't hold on to his visa.

MARGO. Do you think he killed someone?

SULYNN. I wouldn't put it past him. He's probably not even a real doctor. And I'll bet anything he saw this coming and tried to cover himself with this restaurant thing, you know, like an escape hatch. But he and Clark have had a lot of trouble with the seller and getting the budget right, one thing after another. I tell you, I've been going nuts. I told Clark what you found out — you know, spouse to spouse — and the two of us went to work on Lars the other night.

MARGO. Look, I hope you didn't reveal anything I told you to Lars.

SULYNN. Of course not. Clark was trying to pin him down about the restaurant, and, of course, he had to tell us that he's going back to Sweden. He told us the only way he can stay is if he marries an American citizen.

MARGO. Well, he'd better hope they legalize gays marrying in this country real soon.

SULYNN. He won't even admit he's gay, so how is it that you think he'd up and marry one? I mean, it took everything Clark and I had to keep from laughing in his face. But then he said he's got access to many more funds than he was originally willing to put into the restaurant, and he'd put everything he had into the restaurant and push the deal through if somehow we could arrange for him to stay here.

MARGO. I don't know how you're going to do that. I remember Harry trying to help a girl who worked in his office. Immigration's tough, even if you know someone who works there. Maybe I could ask Harry for advice. This girl Elena still works for him, so he must have been able to pull some strings.

SULYNN. Margo, Harry can't help Lars, and he can't help us. But you could.

MARGO. Sulynn, how can I help the guy? Short of marrying him . . . woman, have you lost your mind?

SULYNN. Margo, stay calm and just hear what I've got to say. He'll drop a huge amount of money on you. And it will set Clark up in this business, and with all this money behind it, they'll make a go of it. Then you can get divorced.

MARGO. Honest to God, Sulynn, I really think you've gone off the deep end. I'm already divorced. I most certainly am not marrying some gay guy so he can stay in the country. I don't care how much money's involved. How could you even ask me to do it?

SULYNN. I'd do it for you.

MARGO. Get real, Sulynn. You would not marry someone you didn't love, someone you couldn't have a real relationship with.

SULYNN. To help you out, I would do it. You can't doubt that.

MARGO. I doubt it totally. Have you thought this through? What about my parents? They'll kill me if I get married again.

SULYNN. Your parents! What in hell do you care what your parents say? You're twenty-five years old. Besides, they don't have to know anything.

MARGO. No, but what will they think when I'm divorced a second time?

SULYNN. You don't have to ever get divorced, you

know. Unless you meet someone you want to marry. And that's not going to happen, and you know why as well as I do. You're still in love with Art. So I say, marry this guy and take the money and have affairs. You could do worse than be known as Mrs. Dr. Lars Andersen. Lots worse. You're not worried about what your parents will say. You're worried about Art. You're being really stupid.

MARGO. Even if I agreed to do this, which I'm not going to do, what about Lars? Is this what he wants? And if he does, why doesn't he ask me himself? What are you, his procurer?

SULYNN. He asked me if you'd be interested, that's all. If I tell him you are, of course, he'll discuss it with you. But I think he was afraid you'd turn him down.

MARGO. That isn't it. He doesn't like to get his hands dirty and talk about uncouth things like money. He's a big phony.

SULYNN. All I ask is that you think it over. And remember, Art isn't worth wasting your time worrying about. Believe me.

MARGO. I'm starved, but I can see I'm not going to get out of here until you tell me the latest gossip about him, so let's get it over with now. Is he marrying Corinne? Is that it?

SULYNN. I wouldn't tell you ordinarily, but it's obvious from this conversation you're still hung up on him, and you've got to get on with your life.

MARGO. By marrying a homosexual so your husband can open a restaurant. Thanks for the concern. What about Art?

SULYNN. He has a new girlfriend, and they're living together.

MARGO. He didn't waste any time. Of course, he didn't think I wasted any time either. You know, of course, he's doing it out of jealousy. He's jealous of the fact that I was linked to Lars in the columns. But I bet what really annoyed him was seeing our picture in the papers.

SULYNN. Don't kid yourself, Margo. He doesn't care what you do, or what you think, and the sooner you understand that, the better off you'll be. You can hate me for being selfish, Margo, but no matter what you do, admit to yourself you've got to let go of Art.

MARGO. I feel a lecture coming on. Let's go and eat. I need my strength.

NOTES

LIBRARY
ST. LOUIS COMMUNITY COLLEGE
AT FLORISSANT VALLEY

An Invitation

Most of the monologues in this volume were written by actors and actresses, based on real-life events. We invite you to tell us your story for publication in future volumes of *By Actors, For Actors*. All types of material are welcome. If you are concerned about your writing style, just write in stream of consciousness. Or just dictate the material onto a cassette and send that along. Editing will shape and focus the material for the performers to use. Selections from unpublished plays may also be submitted. Please be sure to include your name, address including zip code, telephone number(s) and social security number. Send all submissions to: Excalibur Publishing, 434 Avenue of the Americas, Suite 790, New York, NY 10011, Attn: By Actors, For Actors. Include a stamped, self-addressed envelope if you want the material returned to you. For Submission Guidelines and compensation information, send a stamped, self-addressed envelope to the same address.

About the Editor

Catherine Gaffigan is a show business professional, with twenty-five years devoted to directing, producing, acting and teaching. As an actress, she made her New York debut opposite Dustin Hoffman in *Journey of the Fifth Horse*. Subsequently, she was seen in summer and winter stock, played Lady MacBeth, and appeared on Broadway in *Whose Life Is It, Anyway?* Her many credits include classical and contemporary plays, film, television commercials, and roles in which she suffered the agonies of soap opera life. She is currently active as a director in New York. Since 1971, Catherine has taught master classes in Acting for Professionals in her own New York studio. She holds a BA in English from St. John's University and an MFA in Drama from The Catholic University of America.